CW00321748

Angels

First published in Great Britain in 1996 by Brockhampton Press,
a member of the Hodder Headline Group, 20 Bloomsbury Street, London WC1B 3QA

This series of little gift books was made by Frances Banfield, Kate Brown, Laurel Clark,
Penny Clarke, Clive Collins, Melanie Cumming, Nick Diggory, Deborah Gill, David Goodman,
Douglas Hall, Maureen Hill, Nick Hutchison, John Hybert, Kate Hybert, Douglas Ingram,
Simon London, Patrick McCreeth, Morse Modaberi, Tara Neill, Anne Newman, Grant Oliver,
Michelle Rogers, Nigel Soper, Karen Sullivan and Nick Wells.

ISBN 1 86019 468 0
A copy of the CIP data is available from the British Library upon request.

Produced for Brockhampton Press by The Flame Tree Publishing,
part of The Foundry Creative Media Company Limited,
The Long House, Antrobus Road, London W4 5HY

Printed and bound in Italy by L.E.G.O. Spa.

CELEBRATION

Angels

Selected by Karen Sullivan

And the angel came in unto her, and said, 'Hail, thou that art highly favoured, the Lord is with thee: blessed art thou among women.' And when she saw him, she was troubled at his saying, and cast in her mind what manner of salutation this should be. And the angel said unto her, 'Fear not, Mary, for thou hast found favour with God. And behold, thou shalt conceive in thy womb and bring forth a son, and you shall call his name Jesus.'

Luke, I:28-31

Angels wear white dresses and have wings and a magic wand. But they only use it if you are good.

Cole, 5

The Love which doth not sleep,
The eternal Arms surround thee:
The Shepherd of the sheep
In perfect love hath found thee.
Sleep through the holy night,
Christ-kept from snare and sorrow,
Until thou wake to light
And love and warmth tomorrow.

Christina Rossetti, *Holy Innocents*

Angels make wishes come true.

Joleen, 4

 2

They look up, with their pale and sunken faces,
And their look is dread to see,
For they mind you of their angels in high places,
With eyes turned on Deity! –
'How long,' they say, 'how long, O cruel nation,
Will you stand, to move the world, on a child's heart, –
Stifle down with a mailed heel its palpitation,
And tread onward to your throne amid the mart?
Our blood splashes upward, O gold-heaper,
And your purple shows your path!
But the child's sob in the silence curses deeper
Than the strong man in his wrath.'

Elizabeth Barrett Browning

Sleep, little Baby, sleep;
The holy Angels love thee,
And guard thy bed, and keep
A blessed watch above thee.
No spirit can come near
Nor evil beast to harm thee:
Sleep, Sweet, devoid of fear
Where nothing need alarm thee.

Traditional lullaby

I Dreamt a Dream! what
   can it mean?
And that I was a maiden
   Queen:
Guarded by an Angel
   mild;
Witless woe, was near
   beguil'd!

William Blake, *The Angel*

The late medieval humanist Johanne Tinctoris noted that when painters wished to show their joy in heavenly things they painted angelic musicians. This motif became popular early in the Renaissance. Angels are shown singing in choirs and playing on contemporary instruments. These are depictions of angels in their heavenly state. Their music is played for the glory of God. As the Psalm says, 'They praise in chords and with organ'. Their music is also dedicated to the Virgin Mary; depictions of the Coronation of the Virgin, such as Fra Angelico's, include hosts of angelic musicians. ... Angelic musicians held for the promise that heaven would in some respects correspond to the world people lived in ...

James Underhill, *Angels*

And now 'twas like all instruments,
Now like a lonely flute;
And now it is an angel's song,
That makes the heavens be mute.

Samuel Taylor Coleridge, *The Rime of the Ancient Mariner*

The mystery of the seven stars which thou sawest in my right hand, and the seven golden candlesticks. The seven stars are the angels of the seven churches: and the seven candlesticks which thou sawest are the seven churches.

Revelations, I:20

The angel of death has been abroad throughout the land; you may almost hear the beating of his wings.

John Bright, in the House of Commons, 23 February, 1855

Every blade of grass has its Angel that bends over it and whispers,
'Grow, grow.'

The Talmud

Every morn from hence
A brisk Cherub something sips
Whose sacred influence
Adds sweetness to his sweetest Lips.
Then to his music. And his song
Tastes of this Breakfast all day long.

Richard Crashaw, *The Weeper*

In poetry, no less than in life, he is a beautiful and ineffectual angel,
beating in the void, his luminous wings in vain.

Matthew Arnold of Shelley, *Essays on Criticism*

How sweet the moonlight sleeps on this bank!
Here will we sit, and let the sounds of music
Creep in our ears: soft stillness and the night
Become the touches of sweet harmony.
Sit, Jessica: look, how the floor of heaven
Is thick inlaid with patines of bright gold:
There's not the smallest orb which thou behold'st
But in his motion like an angel sings,
Still quiring to the young-eyed cherubins.

William Shakespeare, *The Merchant of Venice*

And with the morn those Angel faces smile,
Which I have loved long since, and lost awhile.

Cardinal Newman, *Lead Kindly Light*

How fading are the joys we dote upon!
Like apparitions seen and gone.
But those which soonest take their flight
Are the most exquisite and strong –
Like angels' visits, short and bright;
Mortality's too weak to bear them long.

John Norris, *The Parting*

Angels live on top of the clouds.

Matthew, 4

Where the bright Seraphim in burning row
Their loud up-lifted Angel trumpets blow.

John Milton, *At a Solemn Music*

Be not forgetful to entertain strangers: for thereby some have
entertained angels unawares.

Hebrews, XIII:2

And yet a spirit still, and bright
With something of an angel light.

William Wordsworth, *She Was a Phantom of Delight*

There are two angels, that attend unseen
Each one of us, and in the great books record
Our good and evil deeds. He who writes down
The good ones, after every action closes
His volume, and ascends with it to God.
The other keeps his dreadful day-book open
Till sunset, that we may repent; which doing,
The record of the action fades away,
And leave a line of white across the page.

Henry Wadsworth Longfellow, *Christus*

What angel wakes me from my flowery bed?

William Shakespeare, *A Midsummer Night's Dream*

In this dim world of clouding cares,
We rarely know, till 'wildered eyes
See white wings lessening up the skies,
The angels with us unawares.

Gerald Massey, *Ballad of Babe Christabel*

[In Heaven are] the archangels who are above angels ... and the angels who are appointed over seasons and years, the angels who are over rivers and sea, and who are over the fruits of the earth, and the angels who are over every grass, giving food to all, to every living thing, and the angels who write all the souls of men ...; in their midst are six Phoenixes and six Cherubim and six six-winged ones continually with one voice singing ...

The Book of the Secrets of Enoch, XIX:3

 23

Angels and ministers of grace defend us!

William Shakespeare, *Hamlet*

It came upon the midnight clear,
That glorious song of old,
From Angels bending near the earth
To touch their harps of gold:
'Peace on earth, good will to man
From Heaven's all gracious King.'
The world in solemn stillness lay
To hear the angels sing.

Edmund Hamilton Sears, *The Angels' Song*

Angels are special.

Tom, 4

Swing low, sweet chariot–
Comin' for to carry me home;
I looked over Jordan and what
did I see?
A band of angels comin' after
me–
Comin' for to carry me home.

American spiritual

At the round earth's imagined
corners, blow
Your trumpets, Angels, and arise,
arise.

John Donne, *Holy Sonnets*

25

During the retreat from Mons in August 1914, the Old Contemptibles were sorely pressed, having suffered heavy losses, and that they had survived at all was attributed by some to divine intervention. Arthur Machen, a journalist, described with great vividness St George and the angels who, clad in white, with flaming swords held back the might of the German First Army. The Angel of Mons became a source of inspiration for battle-weary troops throughout the remainder of the war.

I love to hear the story
Which angel voices tell.

Emily Miller, *The Little Corporal*

Of sunbeams, shadows, butterflies, and birds
Angels and winged creatures that are lords
Without restraint of all which they behold

William Wordsworth, *Home at Grasmere*

Matthew, Mark, Luke, and John,
Bless the bed that I lie on,
Four angels to my bed,
Four angels round my head,
One to watch, and one to pray,
And two to bear my soul away.

Thomas Ady

Hush! my dear, lie still and slumber,
Holy angels guard thy bed!
Heavenly blessings without number
Gently falling on thy head.

Isaac Watts, *Cradle Hymn*

Muslim tradition holds that angels were created from pure bright gems; the genii from fire; and man from clay.

Goodnight, sweet prince,
And flights of angels sing thee to thy rest!

William Shakespeare, *Hamlet*

Legend has it that Pope Gregory the Great (590-604) saw some fair-haired youths in the slave market in Rome and asked where they had come from. He was told they were Angles, and also heathens. 'Not Angles, but angels,' he observed, and arranged for St Augustine to journey to Britain to effect their conversion to Christianity.

Ye holy angels bright
Who wait at God's right hand,
Or through the realms of light
Stream at your Lord's command,
Assist our song,
For else the theme
Too high doth seem
For mortal tongue.

Richard Baxter, *Ye Holy Angels Bright*

Angels are like fairies.

Alex, 4

... The feet of angels bright;
Unseen they pour blessing
And joy without ceasing
On each bud and blossom
And each sleeping bosom.

William Blake, *Night*

For fools rush in, where angels fear to tread.

Alexander Pope, *An Essay on Criticism*

'Tis strange what a man may do, and a woman
yet think him an angel.

W.M. Thackeray, *Henry Esmond*

I think that angels spend their time in the holy land serving Jesus.

Tom, 7

When a man's soul and a woman's soul unite together
– that makes an angel.

D.H. Lawrence

You may not be an angel
'Cause angels are so few,
But until the day that one comes along
I'll string along with you.

Al Dubin, *Twenty Million Sweethearts*

Tears such as angels weep burst forth.

John Milton, *Paradise Lost*

Its visits,
Like those of angels, short, and far between.

Robert Blair

Thou fair-hair'd angel of the evening,
Now, whilst the sun rests on the mountains, light
Thy bright torch of love.

William Blake, *To the Evening Star*

And the Sons of Mary smile and are blessèd – they know the Angels
are on their side.
They know in them is the Grace confessèd, and for them are the
Mercies multiplied.
They sit at the Feet – they hear the Word – they see how truly the
Promise runs.
They have cast their burden upon the Lord, and – the Lord He lays it
on Martha's Sons!

Rudyard Kipling, *Martha's Sons*

And he dreamed, and behold a ladder set up on the earth, and the top of it reached to heaven: and behold the angels of God ascending and descending on it.

Genesis, XXVIII:12

The virtue of angels is that they cannot deteriorate; their flaw is that they cannot improve. Man's flaw is that he can deteriorate; and his virtue is that he can improve.

Hasidic saying

I think angels live with God. I think angels can do magic.

Benjamin, 6

Whether the angels
play only Bach in
praising God I am not
quite sure; I am sure,
however, that en
famille they play
Mozart.

Karl Barth

The Lovers took within this ancient grove
Their last embrace; beside those crystal springs
The Hermit saw the Angel spread his wings
For instant flight; the Sage in yon alcove
Sate musing; on that hill the Bard would rove,
Not mute, where now the linnet only sings:
Thus everywhere to truth Tradition clings,
Or Fancy localises Powers we love.
Were only History licensed to take note
Of things gone by, her meagre monuments
Would ill suffice for persons and events:
There is an ampler page for man to quote,
A reader book of manifold contents,
Studied alike in palace and in cot.

William Wordsworth, *Fancy and Tradition*

Angels can fly because they take themselves lightly.

G.K. Chesterton, *Orthodoxy*

And, whilst that slow sure Angel which aye stands
Watching the beck of Mutability
Delays to execute her high commands,
And, though a nation weeps, spares thine and thee.

Percy Bysshe Shelley, *To the Lord Chancellor*

From one piece of wood one can carve an angel or a devil.

Jewish proverb

My great, great, great, great Aunt is an angel.

Isabel, 7

They are idols of hearts and of households;
They are angels of God in disguise;
The sunlight that sleeps in their tresses,
His glory still gleams in their eyes;
These truants from home and from Heaven.
They have made me more manly and mild;
And I know now how Jesus could liken
The kingdom of God to a child.

Charles Monroe Dickinson, *The Children*

Perhaps some saints in glory guess the truth,
Perhaps some angels read it as they move,
And cry one to another full of ruth,
'Her heart is breaking for a little love.'
Though other things have birth,
And leap and sing for mirth,
When springtime wakes and clothes and feeds the earth.

Yet saith a saint: 'Take patience for thy scathe.'
Yet saith an angel: 'Wait, for thou shalt prove
True best is last, true life is born of death,
O thou, heart-broken for a little love.
Then love shall fill thy girth,
And love make fat thy dearth,
When new spring builds new heaven and clean new earth.'

Christina Rossetti

Around our pillows golden ladders rise,
And up and down the skies,
With winged sandals shod.
The angels come, and go, the Messengers of God.

Richard Henry Soddard, *Hymn to the Beautiful*

They can fly to heaven.
They are kind.
They have got wings.
They can sing.
They wear white dresses.

Tom, 6

This miserable state [Virgil informs Dante] is endured by the dreary souls of those who lived without blame and without praise. They are mingled with the cowardly choir of angels who were not rebellious, nor were loyal to God, but were for themselves. Heaven drove them forth to keep its splendour from being sullied; and the depths of hell receives them not, for the wicked would thus have some glory over them ... The world allows no report of them to exist. Mercy and justice disdain them. Let us not speak of them; but look thou and pass. ... And I looked and saw a swirling banner that went by so quickly that it seemed as if it would never pause; and behind it came so long a train of people that I should never have believed death had undone so many ... These wretches, who were never truly alive, were naked and viciously stung ...

Dante, *Inferno* III:34–69

But if she sang or if she spoke,
'Twas music soft and grand,
As though a distant singing sea
Broke on a tuneful strand;
As though a blessed Angel were singing a glad song,
Halfway between earth and heaven.

Christina Rossetti, *Eleanor*

Now walk the angels on the walls of heaven,
As sentinels to warn th'immortal souls,
To entertain divine Zenocrate.

Christopher Marlowe

They are ever reading;
and that never passes
away which they read;
for by choosing, and by
loving, they read the very
unchangeableness of Thy
counsel. Their book is
never closed, nor their
scroll folded up.

Confessions of St Augustine

Angels are special at Christmas and they took my teeth and gave me two one-pounds and a fifty pence.

Hannah, 4

By philosophy man realizes the virtual characteristics of his race. He attains the form of humanity and progresses on the hierarchy of beings until in crossing the straight way (or 'bridge') and the correct path, he becomes an angel.

Brethren of Purity, *Risalat Al-Jami'ah*

Passing beyond the teachings of Angels, the soul goes on to the knowledge and understanding of things, no longer merely betrothed but dwelling with the bridegroom.

Clement of Alexandria

... and whatsoever you see of spiritual forms and of things visible whose countenance is godly to behold and whatsoever you see of thought, imagination, intelligence, soul and the heart with its Secret and whatsoever you see of Angelic aspect, or things whereof Satan is the spirit ... Lo, I, the Perfect Man, am that whole, and that whole is my theatre ... The sensible world is mine, and the Angel world is of my weaving and fashioning.

Abdul Karim Jili, *The Perfect Man*

Then I looked, and I heard the voice of many angels surrounding the throne and the living creatures and the elders; they numbered myriads of myriads and thousands of thousands.

Revelations, V:11

Happy those early days! when I
Shin'd in my angel-infancy.
Before I understood this place
Appointed for my second race,
Or taught my soul to fancy aught
But a white celestial thought.

Henry Vaughan, *The Retreat*

Their garments are white, but with an unearthly whiteness. I cannot
describe it, because it cannot be compared to earthly whiteness; it is
much softer to the eye. These bright Angels are enveloped in a light so
different from ours that by comparison everything else seems dark.
When you see a band of fifty you are lost in amazement. They seem
clothed with golden plates, constantly moving, like so many suns.

Père Lamy

... every one had four wings. And their feet were straight feet; and the sole of their feet was like the sole of a calf's foot; and they sparkled like the colour of burnished brass. And they had the hands of a man under their wings on their four sides ... Their wings were joined to one another ... As for the likeness of their faces, they four had the face of a man, and the face of a lion, on the right side; and they four had the face of an ox on the left side; they four also had the face of an eagle.

Ezekiel, I: 4–10

Take care that you do not despise one of these little ones, for I tell you, in heaven their angels continually see the face of my Father.

Matthew, XVIII:10

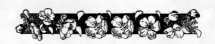

Two words, indeed, of praying we remember,
And at midnight's hour of harm,
'Our Father,' looking upward in the chamber,
We say softly for a charm.
We know no other words, except 'Our Father,'
And we think that, in some pause of angels' song,
God may pluck them with the silence sweet to gather,
And hold both within His right hand which is strong.
'Our Father!' If He heard us, He would surely
(For they call Him good and mild)
Answer, smiling down the steep world very purely,
'Come and rest with Me, My child.'

Elizabeth Barrett Browning

Angels shine from without because their spirits are lit from within by
the light of God.

Traditional country saying

If we could speak with the tongues of angels, our first word would always be God.

Anonymous

Angels need not wings for they soar on the currents of love –
everlastingly.

Anonymous

Angels and archangels, cherubim and seraphim, powers and
principalities: Are they different kinds of angels or just job
descriptions?

The Angel's Little Instruction Book

[The angel] tapped Peter on the side, and woke him, saying, 'Get up
quickly.' And the chains fell off his wrists. The angel said to him,
'Fasten your belt and put on your sandals.' He did so. Then he said to
him, 'Wrap your cloak around you and follow me.'

Acts, XII:7–8

 70

... it was the angels who uplifted our illustrious ancestors towards the divine, and they did so by prescribing roles of conduct, by turning them from wandering and sin to the right way of truth, or by coming to announce and explain sacred orders, hidden vision or transcendent mysteries, or divine prophecies ...'

Dionysius, bishop of Athens, 1st century AD

In heaven an angel is nobody in particular.

George Bernard Shaw

Angels at the foot,
And Angels at the head,
And like a curly little lamb
My pretty babe in bed.

Christina Rossetti

No child is born a criminal: no child is born an angel: he's just born.

Sir Sydney Smith

The Lord, before whom I walk, will send his angel with you and make your way successful.

Genesis, XXIV:40

Now tell the poor young children, O my brothers,
To look up to Him and pray;
So the blessèd One who blesseth all the others,
Will bless them another day.
They answer, 'Who is God that He should hear us,
While the rushing of the iron wheels is stirred?
When we sob aloud, the human creatures near us
Pass by, hearing not, or answer not a word.
And *we* hear not (for the wheels in their resounding)
Strangers speaking at the door:
Is it likely God, with angels singing round Him,
Hears our weeping any more?'

Elizabeth Barrett Browning

The glorious image of the Maker's beauty,
My sovereign saint, the idol of my thought,
Dare not henceforth above the bounds of duty
To accuse of pride, or rashly blame for aught.
For, being as she is divinely wrought,
And of the brood of angels heavenly born,
And with the crew of blessed saints upbrought,
Each of which did her with their gifts adorn,
The bud of joy, the blossom of the morn,
The beam of light, whom mortal eyes admire,
What reason is it then but she should scorn
Base things, that too her love too bold aspire?
Such heavenly forms ought rather worshipped be,
Than dare be loved by men of mean degree.

William Shakespeare, *Sonnets*

And lo, a sudden brightness flooded the great forest on all sides, so bright that it set me on doubt if it were lightning ... A little farther on, a delusive semblance of seven trees of gold was caused by the long space that still intervened between us and them; but when I had drawn nigh ... distinguished them as candlesticks ... Then I beheld people clad in white following after them as after their leaders and whiteness so pure as there never was on earth ... When I was at a point on the bank where only the river separated me from them ... I saw the flames, which seemed like streaming banners, advance, leaving the air behind them panting ... Beneath so fair a sky as I describe came four and twenty elders, two by two, crowned with lilies ... Even as star follows star in the heavens, four creatures came after them, each crowned with green leaves. Every one was plumed with six wings, the plumes full of eyes ... The space between these four contained a triumphal car upon two wheels, which came drawn at the neck of a griffin ...

Dante, *Purgatorio* XXIX:16–143

Look homeward, Angel, now, and melt with ruth.

John Milton

Angels must have a great time in heaven.

Lucie, 7

Whether we see them or not, God's angels are always sent to us in answer to our prayers.

The Angel's Little Instruction Book

Angel
Pure
So
Clean
Because
All
Your
Sins
Have
Been
Washed
Away
Tenderly

Bathed
By
His
Own
Pure
Hand
Angel
Will
You
Cleanse
Me?

Kitty Browne

Notes on Illustrations

Page viii *Cupid Inspiring the Plants with Love*, by Philip Reinagle (Fitzwilliam Museum, University of Cambridge). Courtesy of The Bridgeman Art Library; **Page 3** *Benedicite No.1 'O All Ye Green Things Upon Earth'*, by Edward A. Fellowes Prynne (Russell-Cotes Art Gallery and Museum, Bournemouth). Courtesy of The Bridgeman Art Library; **Page 5** *Angels at the Annunciation*, by Francesco Granacci (Galleria Dell' Accademia, Florence). Courtesy of The Bridgeman Art Library; **Page 6-7** Stowe, Bucks: *Detail of Decoration from the Pompeian Music Room*, designed, by Vincenzo Valdre (Photo Credit: John Bethell). Courtesy of The Bridgeman Art Library; **Page 8-9** *The Birth of Venus*, by Sandro Botticelli (Galleria Degli Uffizi, Florence). Courtesy of The Bridgeman Art Library; **Page 10** *Benedicite No.2 'All That Move in the Water'*, by Edward A. Fellowes Prynne (Russell-Cotes Art Gellery and Museum, Bournemouth). Courtesy of The Bridgeman Art Library; **Page 13** *The Angel of Life*, by Giovanni Segantini. (Galleria D'Arte Moderna, Milan). Courtesy of The Bridgeman Art Library; **Page 15** *Two Angels*, by Charles François Sellier (Private Collection). Courtesy of The Bridgeman Art Library; **Page 18-19** *Putti Disporting*, by Luca Giordano (The Trustees of The Weston Park Foundation). Courtesy of The Bridgeman Art Library; **Page 10** *An Angel Holding a Glass Flask*, by Juan de Valdes Leal (Phillips, The International Fine Art Auctioneers, London). Courtesy of The Bridgeman Art Library; **Page 22** *Venus and Cupid*, by Marco and Sebastiano Ricci (Chiswick House, London). Courtesy of The Bridgeman Art Library; **Page 25** *Putti Amid Swags of Flowers and Leaves*, by Andien de Clermont (Phillips, The International Fine Art Auctioneers, London). Courtesy of The Bridgeman Art Library; **Page 26** *Angel Beating a Drum*, detail from *The Linaivoli Triptych*, by Fra Angelico (Museo Di San Marco Dell'Angelico, Florence). Courtesy of The Bridgeman Art Library; **Page 29** *History of Jove and Io*, by Sebastiano Ricci (Moor Park, Hertfordshire). Courtesy of The Bridgeman Art Library; **Page 30** *The Virgin in Paradise*, by Antoine Auguste Ernest Hebert (Musée Hebert, Paris). Courtesy of The Bridgeman Art Library; **Page 32-3** *Putti Disporting*, by Luca Giordano (The Trustees of The Weston Park Foundation). Courtesy of The Bridgeman Art Library; **Page 34** *Madonna of the Rocks*: detail of the *Head of the Angel*, by Leonardo da Vinci (National Gallery, London). Courtesy of The Bridgeman Art Library; **Page 37** *Benedicite No.2 'All That Move in the Water'*, by Edward A. Fellowes Prynne (Russell-Cotes Art Gallery and Museum, Bournemouth). Courtesy of The Bridgeman Art Library; **Page 39** Advertising Poster for Circular Pointed Pens made, by C. Bradauer & Co (Dickens House Museum, London). Courtesy of The Bridgeman Art Library; **Page 42-3** *Angel Feeding a Peacock,* detail from *The Journey of the Magi Cycle in the Chapel*, by Benozzo di Lese di Sandro (Palazzo Medici-Riccardi, Florence). Courtesy of The Bridgeman Art Library;

Page 45 *A Vision*, by William Edward Frost (Moss Galleries, London). Courtesy of The Bridgeman Art Library; **Page 47** *Benedicite No.4 'O All Ye Fowls of the Air'*, by Edward A. Fellowes Prynne (Russell-Cotes Art Gallery and Museum, Bournemouth). Courtesy of The Bridgeman Art Library; **Page 48-9** Stowe, Bucks: *Detail of the Pompeian Music Room Wall* designed & painted, by Vincenzo Valdre (Photo Credit: John Bethell). Courtesy of The Bridgeman Art Library; **Page 51** *Cupid Sharpening his Arrow*, by Charles Joseph Natoire (Hermitage, St Petersburg). Courtesy of The Bridgeman Art Library; **Page 55** *Angel Blowing Trumpet*, by Lavinia Hamer (Private Collection). Courtesy of The Bridgeman Art Library; **Page 56** Detail from *The Nativity*, by Francesco Giorgio Martini (San Domenico, Siena). Courtesy of The Bridgeman Art Library; **Page 58-9** *Venus at her Toilet*, by The Fontainebleau School (Louvre, Paris). Courtesy of Lauros-Giraudon and The Bridgeman Art Library; **Page 60** *Putti with Garlands of Flowers*, by Charles Robinson (Private Collection). Courtesy of The Bridgeman Art Library; **Page 63** *Swarm of Cherubs, a Group of Children in the Sky*, by Jean-Honore Fragonard (Louvre, Paris). Courtesy of Giraudon and The Bridgeman Art Library; **Page 67** *Trinity with St Ursula & St Margaret*, by Antonio Maria Viani (Location Unknown). Courtesy of The Bridgeman Art Library; **Page 68-9** *Putti Disporting*, by Luca Giordano (The Trustees of The Weston Park Foundation). Courtesy of The Bridgeman Art Library; **Page 71** *The Siren*, by Armand Point (Barry Friedman, New York). Courtesy of The Bridgeman Art Library; **Page 72** *The Virgin in Paradise*, by Antoine Auguste Ernest Hebert (Musée Hebert, Paris). Courtesy of Giraudon and The Bridgeman Art Library; **Page 74-5** *Seated Nymph with Flutes*, by François Boucher (Wallace Collection, London). Courtesy of The Bridgeman Art Library; **Page 77** *The Toilet of Venus*, by Jean-François Janinet (British Museum, London). Courtesy of The Bridgeman Art Library; **Page 81** *Benedicite No.4 'O All Ye Fowls of the Air'*, by Edward A. Fellowes Prynne (Russell-Cotes Art Gallery and Museum, Bournemouth). Courtesy of The Bridgeman Art Library; **Page 82** *L'Innocence*, by William-Adolphe Bouguereau (Christie's, London). Courtesy of The Bridgeman Art Library.

Acknowledgements: The Publishers wish to thank everyone who gave permission to reproduce the quotes in this book. Every effort has been made to contact the copyright holders, but in the event that an oversight has occurred, the publishers would be delighted to rectify any omissions in future editions of this book. Children's quotes printed courtesy of Herne Hill School; *Angels*, James Underhill, reprinted courtesy of Element Books Limited © Sean Konecky 1994; *The Angel's Little Instruction Book*, extracts reprinted courtesy of Marshall Pickering, an imprint of HarperCollins Publishers; *Purgatorio*, Dante, reprinted courtesy of Sidgwick & Jackson.